Anthony, Mary-Anna and Me

Dolores M. Miller
www.BeautifulWarrior.com
facebook.com/DoloresMMiller

ISBN:
978-0-9817506-9-9

Copyright © 2019 by Dolores M. Miller
All rights reserved. This book or any portion thereof
may not be reproduced or used in any manner whatsoever
without the express written permission of the publisher.
All rights reserved.

Contents

Chapter 1 11
    Starlight time
Chapter 2 15
    Forgiveness
Chapter 3 21
    Moving
Chapter 4 23
    Compassion
Chapter 5 25
    The Dream
Chapter 6 27
    The Funeral
Chapter 7 33
    Reunion - Meeting up again

Forward

Although it began in 2015, the story really begins long before that, in 1950's Philadelphia, East Falls to be exact, where two little girls living in row houses became friends. It was inevitable that we become friends; in that city block, there were few children, and besides, our birthdays were only two days apart. Dolores and I played together nearly every day after school, and all day during the summers. My younger brother, Anthony, was the youngest and only boy in our family of five kids. I was two years older than he and, with my sisters being older, he and I played together often as well, with Dolores as the third partner in crime – hopscotch, army men, store, but mostly school, with Dee and I as the teachers and Anthony as the student, since we were older and wiser.

Those were golden days, never to be replicated, but always thought of with a smile. Although Dee moved to a different section of East Falls, we stayed in touch for a while, but with our going to different high schools, we drifted. We saw each other occasionally, but after my marriage, and then hers, we lost touch.

Fast forward several decades. In my quest to stay in touch after my husband John and I retired and moved from Pennsylvania to Delaware, I finally created a Facebook account so I could be in closer communication with our children and grandchildren. I joined a Facebook page entitled "I'm From East Falls," since I still had much love for this area of the city. As a member of the Archdiocesan Choir of Philadelphia, I return to the city on a regular basis and enjoy driving through East Falls on my way to center city.

On March 21, 2015, on the East Falls Facebook page, I noticed a post by Dolores Miller. Could this person be the Dolores Steinberg that I knew and loved as a child? We began the exchange:

Mary-Anna: Dolores Steinberg?? How are you? Hope all is well.
Dolores: I'm good. I'm an author, poet and inspirational speaker. Where did u live Mary-Anna - on Ridge Avenue?
Dolores: Bonoma?
Mary-Anna: YES! I now live in Rehoboth Beach, Delaware. I'm a retired teacher.
Dolores: I'm going to be writing a book about Anthony
Mary-Anna: Anthony? My brother?
Dolores: I have so many wonderful memories of you both and us playing school.
Mary-Anna: OMG! I'm so excited to hear from you. How wonderful! Let me know if you need anything.
Dolores: Even when I didn't see you guys for years I dreamt I was walking through the house right before Anthony died. The bond never changed from our childhood.
Mary-Anna: I'm totally impressed and happy! So glad to connect with you!
Dolores: I'm crying I'm so happy!
Mary-Anna: Me too!!!
Dolores: ANTHONY IS MY ANGEL.
Mary-Anna: OMG! Now crying even more!
Dolores: OMG!

And so, our second journey began. Dee and I reunited during one of my trips to choir rehearsal, and we continue to do so whenever I'm in the city. We share stories of our childhood and of our lives now, photos of ourselves and our grandchildren, and thoughts on living the good life. We cannot believe our fortune and the grace of God in our

lives. But most of all, we thank God for his blessings in giving us our angel, Anthony, to bring us together again.
Mary-Anna Bonoma Harvie
6 Stafford Road
Rehoboth Beach, DE 19971
215-915-4478
maharvie@yahoo.com

Introduction

Dear Reader,

When I think of our special friendship – a friendship of three children growing up in Pennsylvania – Dolores, Mary-Anna and Anthony, it fills my heart with joy. I want everyone to know of our special friendship which continues today and the lessons we learned through our relationship. We didn't know it then, but that starlight time helped us see the beauty of life, and now we think of those years as beautiful stepping stones, to help us overcome adversities in life.

I want you to know about my true childhood friend Anthony, and what I learned by sharing his story. The love, friendship, kindness, forgiveness and a shared connection - precious times that were like sparkling jewels are transformed into this book called "Anthony, Mary-Anna and Me".

I wish to share this wisdom with you:

- Try to be in your moments, not thinking about "what-if" or worrying about the future.
- Take time to see beauty every day. This world has a lot of harshness - seeing beauty helps you see beyond the harshness.
- Always try to help others who are suffering.
- Remember the people who were in your life when it was most difficult.
- Always be healthy and happy and remember there is always hope!
- In God's eyes, even a hundred years is a very short amount of time. Become all you were meant to be - don't let yourself or others hold you down.
- We don't know how long we have on earth. Don't waste your precious time; if you are

having hard times in the present, don't forget that things will change, and we can always hope for the best!

I am here to tell our story, so I may help others - Anthony had so many years ahead of him, but cancer took him home way too early.

Chapter 1
Starlight time

It was a Starlight time; kids were kids, we played and laughed and sang and danced. In our starlight time, only the classroom and our friendship existed... there was no harshness or pain in that room, just joy and fun; there was no outside world.

I was eight years old and was friends with Mary-Anna and her younger brother Anthony. We were just a few kids playing school in the basement of a row home in Philadelphia.

I asked my mom if I could go to the Bonoma's house. "Mom, can I take the nun outfits to Mary-Anna's now?" I loved the nun outfits – my mom made them! The outfits were exactly like the Saint Joe's nuns from years ago – black robe and veil with a white collar which covers the scalp.

My mom asked if my home homework was done. I assured her it was, and she told me to go ahead, but be careful. I thanked her as I ran out the door. I loved being a being a nun teacher! I couldn't wait to get to my friend's house. As soon as I knocked on the front door, Anthony swung it open and excitedly told me to come in; they were already playing in the basement. As we walked through the living room, we encountered Mr. Bonoma – and as usual, he called out "How are you, fat belly?" We giggled and laughed... even though I was so skinny my belly always stuck out!

I loved to smell the roses – there was always a vase of roses in front of the blessed mother statue in the entryway at the Bonoma's. I would always smell the roses as I walked through the Bonoma's house and savor the smell of gravy (as the Italian's call it) as soon as I walked in the door.

I called out to Mrs. Bonoma – "oh, your gravy smells so good!" Mrs. Bonoma asked "do want me to call your mom and see if you can stay for dinner?" "YES!"

Anthony yelled down the stairs, "Mary-Anna, we're comin' down. You ready?" I loved being in their basement, it was set up like a classroom. There was a chalkboard, old fashioned student desks, an old teacher's desk, textbooks were on the teacher's desk. Chalk, erasers, pens, pencils and paper were always in the room. I can still see Anthony's sweet smile, sitting in his seat like a good student while Mary-Anna and I wore our nun outfits, so we could be the teacher. I loved spending a lot of time at their house and in this classroom.

Almost immediately Mary-Anna starts to argue with me – "I want to be the teacher", I replied "You are ALWAYS the teacher; I want to be the teacher!" I start to argue with Mary-Anna and try to make a deal. "I will be the teacher today - YOU can be the teacher tomorrow." Anthony just hangs in the background, mumbling about not minding being the student – he thinks it is fun to be the student. And of course, Mary-Anna comes back with "Tomorrow you'll say the same thing – tomorrow never comes for me – I'll never get my turn. NO, I will be the teacher today - YOU can be the teacher tomorrow!"

Well, I told HER! "oh yeah, that's how you want it? I'm not playing'. I'M JUST GOING HOME!" I ignored Mary-Anna and started talking to just Anthony. "Anthony, don't you have a game tomorrow?" Anthony replied,

"yeah, in the afternoon – it's good - we won the last couple ga....mes – Mary-Anna is furious and stomps her foot – "Dolores, you are so bossy!"

I put my hands on my hips and really let her have it! "Look whose talkin'" and then Mary-Anna whined at me – "at least I don't whine like a baby when I don't get my own way!" I called her out on it – "BAH – LONE –EEEE. You are just mad, because I am a better teacher – AND my mom

made the nun outfits – they are MINE and I AM GOING HOME!"
Mary-Anna started to give in and begged with her hands - I still want to be the teacher. I told her "NOT TODAY!" I couldn't just back down now. Anthony was always trying to make peace. "Mary-Anna, just leave her alone and let her be the teacher." Mary-Anna declared "Alright, I'll be the teacher's aide today – but I AM TEACHER NEXT TIME!" I had to get the last word – so I gave it to her – "Fine!"
I didn't want to give her a chance to change her mind, so I ushered her in to the nearest desk and gave out the textbooks. I addressed the class and told them to sit in their seats and we'll get started. "Today, we are learning math". I called on Mary-Anna to do some math problems on the board. I wanted her to have some time in front of the classroom – even though I was the teacher. There were a few times when Mary-Anna was the teacher, we took turns, but Anthony was always the student. I can still feel the touch of the real textbooks and the smoothness of the white chalk as the powder stuck to my hands.
We didn't know it then; the hours would just pass, many hours of us playing. I still feel a secure, happy feeling when I think of that starlight time! We were immune to the outside world. We had so many hours of learning, make-believe and pure fun.

Chapter 2
Forgiveness

We attended St. Bridget's School. In the lunchroom, there was a sign for St. Bridget's, a large clock on the wall and a loud bell which started and stopped lunch period. There were always cafeteria workers handing out food and sandwiches or spooning out the hot foods onto our plates and bowls. We would always hear the workers and the lunch moms, "settle down, settle down, THERE IS NO RUNNING IN THE CAFETERIA! Stop Runnnnning!" Mary-Anna and I were eating lunch and Mary-Anna asked if I was going to come over after school. I was not in a good mood. I rolled my eyes and gave her the strongest glare I could, and then I said "no, I won't be over!" and gave her the silent treatment! BIG TIME! Mary-Anna asked "well, are you coming or not?", I stared and acted like she hadn't said a word. Mary-Anna asked, "now what?" I couldn't take it anymore, I wasn't in a good mood, I told her "I don't feel like answering – leave me alone." Mary-Anna looked hurt and I thought she was going to cry, she kept asking "why are you acting this way?", I was mad, and I wanted her to know it. I fired back "Are you still talking?" When I look back now, I really don't know why I was in a bad mood. Mary-Anna did all she could – she shouted, "don't think you are coming over now - you aren't invited!" I waited a good long time, I stared and stared, and then I said, "I'll be there if Anthony wants me to be there." Mary-Anna was quick to come back with "Oh, no you WON'T!" I just laughed at her. I knew Anthony would let me come over. It was as though Mary-Anna read my mind, she yelled back, "you think you are better because he ALWAYS gives into you!". I let Mary-Anna and everyone else in the lunchroom know just how mad I was, I shouted "I am not talking to you!" Mary-Anna hung her head and quietly sobbed and just as she was getting ready to make a retort, the bell rang, and lunch was over – and even if we didn't hear the bell, we knew lunch was over because everyone started to leave, and we could hear the lunch ladies once again yelling in the background "I said NO RUNNING!"

We went back to our class and I couldn't wait for school to be over. I finally got home and sat down to do my homework. And then it hit me… I had to tell my mom I couldn't do my homework, I was so upset about my argument with Mary-Anna that I forgot to pack my book with my homework!

"Mom, I can't do my homework – I left it at schoooolllll", my mom answered by repeating what I said – almost mocking me. "Can't do your homework?", "That's what you think – take your copybook and go ask Mary-Anna." Now, I was gonna get it - I begged my mom "can't you just call her or her mom?", "no and nope, I didn't forget my homework, now move it, move along.", I whined one last plea "mooooommmmmmm" and my mom just continued making dinner while she repeated, "Move it – NOW". I packed my bag and went to the Bonoma's house. With this, I learned I shouldn't burn my bridges. I knocked on the door and Mrs. Bonoma answered. I was a little upset and a little scared, I wasn't sure if Mary-Anna would have told her mom how I acted in school. I was right. As soon as I started to tell Mrs. Bonoma that I forgot my homework, she interrupted me and said, "I heard you weren't very nice to my Mary-Anna today…", I just broke down… I started crying and sobbing. "Yeah, I wasn't". Mrs. Bonoma started kissing away my tears and whispered "It's ok honey". She hugged me tight. Just then Mary-Anna walked in the room and calmly asked "Are you over it yet?" and Mrs. Bonoma reprimanded her daughter with a stern "Mary-Annnnnaaaaaa". Anthony came into the room wearing his baseball uniform. He casually asked, "Now what?" and "Everything ok in here?" In that moment, I learned that just because I'm in a bad mood, I don't have to be mean.

I told him I had a fight with Mary-Anna in school and he ignored it and said "well, are we playin' school or not? I gotta leave soon." Mary-Anna pipped in with "she had her own fight". Mrs. Bonoma reprimanded her again "Mary-ANnnnnnaaaaaa", and Mary-Anna loudly sighed, them said "alright, alright, I get it – yeah let's play" and she sighed again for a slight dramatic affect.

We went to the basement to play school and to let me do my homework. As soon as we got to the bottom step, Mary-Anna said, "let me guess, you will want to be the teaacchheerrrr."

I told her "I guess, no, no, well, I guess, it's time… but I really like being the teacher the best - AND I am good at it – ok, I give, let Anthony be the teacher for today". May Anna started to cry "you just don't want to ever let ME be the teacher!" I saw through the drama and rolled my eyes. Anthony was always the peacemaker and today was no exception. "It's ok Mary-Anna, you teach today. I have baseball soon anyway".

I'd had enough of this teacher nonsense for one day; I looked in their direction and asked, "When you leave we can play Barbie Dolls, OK, Mary-Anna?" "Just to see if we could still play a little longer and Mary-Anna replied, "OK, I am teacher until he leaves!", I replied in the only way I could "whatevvver".

After we finished playing school, we were going to the playground to watch Anthony's game. Anthony kept telling us to "Hurry up guys, we can't be late, the coach will be mad, he likes us to practice before every game." I had to tell him "we're coming, we're coming, you walk too fast." And then Mary-Anna started chiming in for me to hurry, because she wanted to play on the swings.

We finally got to swing on the swings. I was swinging and shouting over to Mary-Anna "This is so fun… look my hair is flying!" Not to be beaten Mary-Anna responded, "I'm higher than you are, look at me kick my legs up", so I did it – I got just as high!

"I am so high, I can see Anthony playing, I hope his team wins – I like playing on the swings, but I think I would like to play baseball too - I'd get to hit the ball and run around all the bases. I bet I could be faster than some of the boys." Mary-Anna told me that was gross "eww, gross! Not me! I wanna swinnnnnnggggggggg!" And then we heard the announcer "And folks, that's the game!" Mary-Anna saw Anthony walking across the fields and shouted, "here comes Anthony."

I asked Anthony as soon as I was jumping off the swing "was it a good game? Did ya win?" Anthony told me they creamed the other team.

On our walk home, I decided it was time to tell Anthony I wanted him to teach me how to play baseball. His reaction was typical – "girls don't play baseball!" I stuck my hands on my hips and belted "Girls can do anything boys can do." He finally agreed and decided we should start with a little game in the back yard.

The first time Anthony threw the ball, I cried out "ow, that hurt, it hit my hand!" Anthony let me use his glove and told me it would be easier to catch. I really just wanted to bat! Soon after Anthony pitched a few balls to me and I struck out on the first two, and then I made a small connect on the third. Anthony fumbled the catch over and over and I was able to make it all the way home. As I was jumping on home plate, I let him know "See, I told you girls can do anything boys can do!"

I was ahead of my time; and a little "woman's libber" even then, still to this day, I don't believe that woman are where they should be! If we wanted to play baseball – we should play baseball.

Usually after school, if we weren't playing school, we played with our Barbie dream house. The Barbie dream house pulled out from a suitcase and unfolded to become a play house - the suitcase opened to make the rooms of the house. We had to assemble our own furniture… it came packed flat and to make something like a dresser or table, you had to insert tab A into slot B. Also, one year, we got our Ken dolls and the Barbie dream car for Christmas! We were so excited! We loved playing with Barbie and Ken and the house and car and pretending we were married. I can still visualize the house and the Christmas tree and playing for hours – we thought we got gold for Christmas!

Chapter 3
Moving

Right after Christmas, my mom explained we were going to be moving soon. I couldn't believe it and I didn't want it. I liked where I lived and my friends and now I would have to leave Anthony and Mary-Anna – my two best friends!
I asked "What?" and I told her "I don't want to move, move, no, no, no."
My mom kept trying to explain, "I know it is hard to leave your friends, but with the new baby we need more room. Don't worry, we'll visit your friends."
I didn't understand why I had to move for a new baby. I asked "Why do I have to move? For that baby?" My mom put her foot down, "Now, you stop that RIGHT now." I ran to my friend's house and I saw the kitchen light was on. I ran up to the door, yelling – "I can't believe it – we are movin'."
Mary-Anna and Anthony heard me, and they start yelling "Dolores is moving!" I started sobbing "We can't play anymore". All three of us were crying holding each other. Mrs. Bonoma came into the kitchen and asked "what's going on here? Why are you yelling?" Anthony tried to speak through his tears – "Dolores is mahmahmahmovin'" Mrs. Bonoma tried to comfort all of us "oh, come here, it will be ok. You can still be friends". Mrs. Bonoma hugged us and wiped our tears. The next day we started packing and getting ready for the big move.
Separating from my friends at such a young age brought up a lot of emotions - I went through sadness and grief after the move, I was missing our times together. I felt the loss. Being a little girl then and moving away from my best friends was very hard. I saw Mary-Anna and Anthony a few more times after the move, but we grew apart. I made new friends with the girls in my new neighborhood and we are still friends to this day; but I always felt a connection to

Mary-Anna and Anthony. I went through my preteens and teens; Anthony and Mary-Anna were always in my heart and mind. They became part of my soul. Moving made me feel like I was in a different world – I think it would have been nice to still be friends with Mary-Anna and Anthony though our teen years! Even now, I daydream of all the fun we would have had together. Years later, I realized we had to move because we didn't have enough room for our expanding family. Anthony and I had mothers who didn't drive, so from age 10 – 16 there was no way to get to each other's houses. When I look back, I was busy with my teenage life and so was Anthony and Mary-Anna. Each of us could have tried harder to see each other.

Chapter 4
Compassion

I learned true compassion; I experienced it with Anthony and his family. Anthony's kindness and love and that of his family became a part of my soul. I loved going to their house. My life has been shaped by sharing that feeling of love, kindness and compassion. I am a minister at heart. When I want to be brought back to that starlight time, I go into a local church and pray, I feel the same calmness and reverence I felt back then…remembering to enjoy all the beautiful things! It helps - even for just those moments to get away from the harshness of this world.

Yesterday, I went to the local church to pray and light candles. My favorite part of church was seeing all the roses and flowers, especially around the baby Jesus. While I was praying, lighting the candles and taking in the view, I noticed there was an older couple in a pew, their distress was obvious, but I continued to pray. I could feel their anguish so clearly and after saying my prayers, I turned around and could undeniably see their pain.

I went over to the woman and held her hand, saying "whatever it is ma'am, it will be ok". She said to me "it will never be ok. We lost two sons in two years." Instantly, I knew I used the wrong words. With such compassion in my heart and a calm and steady voice, I told her "you are right Ma'am it will never be ok, but as time goes on you will learn to live with the pain even as hard as it is". The man reached out and grabbed my hand - he had such a strong handshake. I was strong with him too, showing him there is strength and courage in this world, even when things are so difficult - at this moment I realized I had a gift. I had no problem holding their hands and reaching out to them to show kindness.

Chapter 5
The Dream

Connections are created with people we love - those connections stay even after we leave this world! Anthony, I had a dream – a very vivid dream. I was walking through the Bonoma house, walking down the long hallway to the living room and walking into the kitchen of your childhood home. I was looking around and I had my hand over my mouth… I was afraid I was going to scream! I thought "someone is dying here", "oh God is it Mr. or Mrs. Bonoma?" I felt extreme sadness. I knew someone was dying. The next day, I got a phone call. Even though I already knew… I just remember saying "What, what, I don't understand". "What happened, I don't believe it". "No, no I won't go, I, I, I can't go and see an angel in a coffin!!!" Soon after, I learned the real meaning of my dream. There was a death, but it was not Mr. or Mrs. Bonoma, it was you Anthony! I could not believe it!
I later found out that while Anthony was sitting in a chair in the living room. He told his dad, "I really have a bad cold in my chest, maybe the chemo brought my resistance down. I think we better go to the hospital." Mr. Bonoma answered "Anything you need Anthony, anything you need" as he helped Anthony put on a coat and get settled in the wheelchair, they immediately went to the hospital.
In my dream, I knew it was Anthony, but my heart and mind would not accept it. Since this dream, I had many more connections and dreams and feelings about people and situations even before the event happened. We can connect with the ones we love after they are in heaven. They are our spiritual guides.

Chapter 6
The Funeral

I couldn't bring myself to go to the funeral, but I knew I had to see the family. I needed to go, I needed to be there. I went to the gathering at the Bonoma's house after the funeral and I was surprised no one said anything about me not going to the funeral. Just like when I was a little girl, everyone was very loving and caring.

Several guests who were at the wake told me that everyone could hear Mr. Bonoma wailing – "Anthony, Anthony why did you do this to me? It was too soon, you were too young. It's not supposed to be this way – I'm supposed to go first... my child, my child, my only son..." This was the first time I understood what the saying "heart torn out from their chest" meant! Losing a child is a grief that goes beyond anything anyone can know unless they have been through it! Now, when I look back, I wish I went to the funeral for the sake of Mary-Anna and Mr. & Mrs. Bonoma.

I learned plenty from Anthony's death, more than I could ever write:

- Death closes one door and opens another
- Never give up
- Every day is a blessing
- Don't waste time away from people you love because you are too busy or too proud or for whatever reason.
- Accept life
- Savor moments and rise above adversities
- Don't let hard times keep you down
- Life is short!
- Become all you were meant to be
- While moments go on – value time with you family and friends

- Value moments in the moment because they are gone quickly
- Take time to help others and see beauty
- Help others who are suffering; show compassion and love
- See the beauty around you
- Tell your loved ones how you feel about them.

Death Closes One Door and Opens Another
I realize here on earth is just a visiting place… our home is in heaven. I believe Anthony is an angel in heaven now, just as I believed he was an angel on earth.
Lesson Learned: We are always connected when we love someone. In the past 50 plus years, I've had many experiences where I had dreams or feelings about the other side. I also knew about things that were going to happen in the future. Anthony was the first experience in my dreams. A few years later, I woke up from a sound sleep and knew my cousin Joey died. Recently, I knew my cousin Danny would be gone soon. He went with God. I had an overwhelming feeling in my family room.

Never Give Up
Anthony and his family taught me to never give up! Anthony fought cancer, lost his leg, took care of his mom and finished college – he didn't give up.

Every Day is a Blessing
I learned to not complain about getting older. Anthony was never that fortunate! Each day, week, month and year that I'm here is like a precious jewel; I will continue my mission and be all I was meant to be! Anthony never had the chance to show the world that he was a wonderful, kind and talented human being. Time is a precious jewel.

Wasted Time
Going into the Bonoma's house after the funeral was so very hard. I had mixed emotions. I didn't know how the family was going to react or treat me. Even though I could not bear to see Anthony - as an angel in a coffin, I imagined all kinds of things the family might say to me. "Why are you here now?" "Why weren't you at the funeral?" "You have nerve coming here now". Even with these thoughts in my head and in my mind, I just knew I had to see the family.
Once I got there and it was so different, then I remembered they always accepted me fully. I learned another valuable lesson that day.

Acceptance!
When people love you, really, really love you there is full acceptance of you. Even sharing this now brings a smile to my face and a warm feeling in my heart.
As I sat in the kitchen, I looked over to the door of our make-believe classroom for a couple of moments, I was there again. It was so vivid, like we were there! Such happy feelings at such a hard time! I could see all of us playing – me as the teacher and Mary-Anna and Anthony as the students. As my attention turned to the people in the room with me, I was warmly greeted, and I got a bear hug from Mrs. Bonoma and Mary-Anna.
I remember Mary-Anna saying, "Oh my, I am so glad you could come." I told her "I had to, I just had to." Everyone joined in with the conversation at the kitchen table – everyone except Mr. Bonoma. He waited in the living room and was just staring into space. He was alone. Such heartbreak… I felt his pain, his complete and utter shattering of his soul.
I told everyone how sorry I was that I didn't go to Anthony's funeral…. And I couldn't stop crying. Mary-Anna just told me "I am glad you are here now… I should

have called you when Anthony got sick." I told them about my dream and how I knew something was happening and it was near the end. I had a dream; I was walking through their house. I had a feeling someone was dying - but I never thought it was Anthony.

We continued to cry, hug and hold hands. Mary-Anna didn't think it was so strange, she was recalling how close we were as children. We couldn't really figure out how we had gone for so long without seeing each other. How did we let so many years slip by? Mary-Anna laughed when she recalled talking and laughing with Anthony and how bossy we were… Anthony was always so gentle, and we were very bossy, headstrong girls! At that time, we just had innocence, joy, happiness and love, no age, no sickness, no cancer and no death!

When Anthony's mom got sick, her toes, foot, and leg were amputated due to diabetes. Anthony stopped going to college to care for his mother. After his mother started to heal, Anthony went back to school to finish his degree. Soon after, he went on a golf outing with his father and his leg gave out. He went to the hospital and discovered his left leg was infected with cancer. Immediately, they amputated his left leg. Anthony graduated from college in May 1978, he got pneumonia shortly after Thanksgiving, he was hospitalized in December with cancer in his lungs and he died December 23, 1978.

Savor Moments
In our lifetime, sometimes we will encounter very hard times. Will they make you or break you? It is up to us, it is our choice.

Anthony faced cancer and death while he was so young. It taught me to never give up! While facing very hard adversities in my life, sometimes it would have been easier to quit… Anthony's death taught me that life is short – face whatever it is and rise above!

I want to take back time; if I knew then, what I know now, I would turn back time and see my pal Anthony. My childhood friend - my Angel, I wouldn't have let all those years pass without having some more fun, without playing and sharing more time together, without learning more from my friend. I would have told him, he was such a good friend of mine and I would have told him "I love you." What did I learn Anthony Dear? For the rest of my life, I will not let time go by without a chance to say goodbye… to every person I love.

As I gazed at the basement door that lead to our make-believe classroom. I longed to have more time, more moments, more magic! If only we could have stayed that age and in that time, we could have learned so much more from each other. If I could have stayed at that age and that time - that starlight time - I wouldn't have had to go through so many ups and downs in my adult life.

It was so pleasant, comfortable and fun to just stay playing in the basement, playing Barbie - even arguing and being the teacher and being with my dear childhood friends. What this taught me was that we should always play- even in adult life. Life is always throwing something here or there. You must deal with it.

If I could take back time, I would like to be there again – but I can't I have to deal with the reality of this adult life and its ups and downs.

Dear Reader, take time for fun even in your adult life. If I had one last chance, what would I say to Anthony… my dear, dear friend? I would talk to him. "Anthony, can you hear me? I am sorry I didn't come to your funeral." I imagine he would talk to me and give some sage advice "I will always be here for you, no matter what happens in your life, don't ever give up!" I would remind him he always had courage and strength, and how he taught me so much. He taught me kindness – how to be kind and compassionate. And he taught me how to love.

"I won't give up, I never will…life here can be too short. I don't want to wait until it is too late. Anthony, you will always be my angel and we will meet again. I will always love you my dear, dear friend…"

It was the last time I looked around and saw that mystical place. If I could change the clock, I would have visited Anthony when I could – and not let life get in the way.

I wish someone told me when Anthony was sick! I would have been there to help ease the shock and pain. We would have held hands and said, "it will be alright" even though it wasn't.

Now, in my life, I would not allow this to happen… if I have a dream or a feeling – I will follow through and be there for my friend or family.

My daughter calls it my gift of being clairvoyant, I think it comes from the Holy Spirit – it is a gift to help others, I will be there for any person who needs me.

Anthony, I know you hear me now and I know, that you know, that I would have been there if I knew you were sick. You are my angel now and I am thankful for that! I tell people that I love them all the time… it is important to hear it! Anthony, I am telling you now, I loved our friendship. I am so happy now that Mary-Anna is in my life. My wish is that you will continue to guide us, lead us and watch over us.

Chapter 7
Reunion - Meeting up again

As you read in the FORWARD of this book, Mary-Anna contacted me on the internet of all things! I am so happy that we won't waste any more time! I really enjoyed meeting Mary-Anna before choir practice, seeing her in the choir and having her as a guest of my toy drive party. It has been wonderful; Mary-Anna, where do I begin? The excitement of meeting with you again after so many years has been incredible. I have been writing the story of Anthony for a couple of years, I just got busy with so many things. The book of Anthony is very important, the message of love and friendship and Anthony as our angel must get out to people. I learned so much from our starlight time together!

I hope Mary-Anna knows that her friendship - not just Anthony's – meant so much to me - even though we would argue, and we were strong-willed and stubborn little girls, that didn't change the way I felt about her and our time playing Barbie and our time doing girl things. It always comes back to Anthony – and always learning from him: his love, friendship and kindness. Mary-Anna was very kind and loving too, but not like Anthony, he was very unique. He was an angel then and he is an angel now.

Mary-Anna,
I never thought about how much I could love the church and seeing you in the choir and remembering the beautiful cathedral. It is quite an epiphany! Spirituality was in my life at a very young age. I believe the Holy Spirit was working through me even then! Saint Michael was in my life from an early age too! The cathedral is the place where my son was married. I feel God's spirit so strongly, and when I hear the choir, I can feel it go through my mind, heart and soul. Just knowing someone like you is in it and

singing to our Heavenly Father and his Blessed Son and Holy Spirit, fills my heart with joy and awe.
I was so happy to have you here for my toy drive! I have been having a toy drive party for over ten years to provide toys, and gifts to the children in the care of the Support Center for Child Advocates of Philadelphia. Of course, I love our dinners on Mondays and I love our talks about the book, and our lives now. I never thought we'd be sixty-five – but here we are! We have so many more adventures ahead of us and I am so happy to have met your husband. I love to share things with you and to be together with our families and having so much fun!
Mary-Anna, what am I going to say about celebrating our 65th birthday together? I never thought it would come, I never thought I would see you again. But as you know, Anthony sent you back into my life, so we could be together for the rest of our lives. Celebrating our 65th birthday together was so exciting! I want you to get to know my friends and I want them to get to know you and let them know about the wonderful woman that I know – and all about our special childhood! Our birthday was a blast with the beautiful cakes and everyone singing Happy Birthday to us!

A few days after our party, I received a birthday message from Mary-Anna:
"My birthday has always been a special day for me. When I was a little girl, my mom would always make a heart-shaped white cake since my birthday is near Valentine's Day, it always had pink-tinted frosting and coconut sprinkled on top, because I have never liked chocolate, and there was always a party for me and my friends. I still like to celebrate my birthday with family and friends. My latest birthday became even more special because you and I reconnected, and we celebrated our birthdays together".
Dee's birthday is the 16th and mine the 18th, so we've

always had that connection as well. But this past year, Dee and I celebrated at Serafina's restaurant, to which she and I would often go when I come to choir rehearsals in Philadelphia. Many of Dee's friends came as well, so we had a huge celebration. "The restaurant was filled with people, balloons, laughter, and conversations, such a festive atmosphere. We even had two cakes, one for her and one for me. Cameras flashed, voices joined in singing "happy birthday," and hands clapped joyfully! We laughed and laughed. We walked back to your home, talking the entire way about what a great day we had had, and how blessed we were to have found each other again".

The Neighborhood
A few months later, we went to visit our old neighborhood from when we were children. It was great to see our old neighborhood and thinking about the time we spent with Anthony. First, we went to the Trolley Café – which was the Old Batley of East Falls - when we were little, it was a swimming pool. Now it is a café. We went to visit both Haywood and Krail streets. It was a wonderful and exciting experience.
The streets look the same, except for Bushhill; it was all bushes and had an old, haunted house, - well, we always thought it was a haunted house. One day, I was going through Bushhill and it scared me a little. I was at the haunted house, and I saw boys sniffing glue out of a paper bag. I was only 11 or 12 years old, it was scary, and the house always seemed haunted - now it is a row of townhouses. Also, we saw Tim Gramlick - he was a friend of my brother Michael (they are about six years younger than us) and he told me how wild they were and how they carried on drinking and having parties and stuff. A few years ago, his wife told him "shape up or ship out" and so he stopped drinking – I think it was very brave of him.

As we walked down the street, Tim started pointing out all the families with five or more kids on that block. It was a catholic neighborhood and some families even had more than five kids. Many of the families were practicing Catholics and didn't use birth control. It was a very close-knit neighborhood. That is what was important about it and what I loved about it. I lived at the corner of Haywood and Krail Street at 3600 Krail Street. And then I saw one of Summer's sons go into the house where I lived as a child. I started remembering a lot of things, like how daddy had the loudspeakers out at Christmas with Perry Como. It was a great memory.

We met with the East Falls paper for an interview – it was exciting – we talked about our childhood and my book about Anthony. And we also went to our old houses that were on the Ridge. We took a picture of me in front of 4062 Ridge Avenue – my old house. Then we went down to Mary-Anna's house, it was four houses away. When I was little, I thought it was so far away, but it really wasn't. My house looks a little like it did, but Maryann's house doesn't. Ridge Avenue has changed - we saw the back of the houses and now new millenniums and yuppies live there. They put little porches on top of the back of the houses. We met a young man and we told him how it was when we were kids. The fields in the back were all open and now there is so much grass back there you can't see anything.

The railroad was right behind the houses. We weren't allowed back there because of the trains; our parents were very strict. Mary-Anna's house had a door where the window used to be. My house still had a porch, but a new door and it was so different, and so exciting at the same time – we could still visualize how our house was when we were little girls.

We looked at the house for Mr. Crezziano, he had a little store there where he sold food, cut lunchmeat and sold

Italian rolls. Mr. Crezziano took in my dad when he had nowhere else to live. The whole block is mostly Italian. Even now 53 years later that starlight time shared with Anthony and Mary-Anna is implanted in my heart and mind.

"Anthony, now I am 65 years old and during my lifetime I saw a lot of misery and joy… but it will never be like the moments we had… moments of sheer friendship and starlight times. I'm so glad I have a connection with Mary-Anna, she has become an unexpected joy in the fall of my life."

My heart aches for our connection; I wonder what it would be like if you were still here. Just like with Mary-Anna, we'd meet up on Facebook and other social media. Maybe you would be married, have kids and grandkids. Or maybe you would have been a priest. Either way, you would have been great at it! And we would have been the best friends ever! Anthony, I think of you and talk to you often… here is one of the letters I've written for you:

Dear Anthony,
If you were here on earth, you would still be one of my best friends. You are in heaven and Mary-Anna and I have you as our angel - you will always be in our hearts and souls. I have become your voice. There were so many years of happy, playful times. Our childhood was a mystical, joyful time, full of love. It was a time when there were no adversities. There was only playing and sharing and fun. We didn't know about the harshness in the world. As I grew up and needed to face adversities, I would think about our starlight time. Anthony and Mary-Anna, you taught me the true meaning of friendship.
There was always complete acceptance of the other person's character. Even today, it is still vivid, my dream of your death was not only seeing and feeling but knowing!

This is one of the first visions or knowings I had... I believe it is a gift! I still have dreams and "knowings" to this day. I often wonder what you would say to me. I imagine it would be something like this: "I will always be here for you, no matter what happens in your life, don't ever give up! I am here now to tell you I will always be your angel. I am walking on holy ground. We can let go of any regrets, we will meet again in paradise."

Anthony, I want you to know everything I didn't get a chance to tell you while you were alive. I wish that we didn't lose time the way we did... What happened? The years went by so fast, one minute we were children, the next, we were adults. I know you are still connected to me because our bond was always so strong. Those memories always put a smile on my face.

Anthony, you always had courage and strength, you taught me so much. You taught me kindness and compassion. And you taught me how to love.

I won't give up, I never will...life here can be too short. I don't want to wait until it is too late. You left me with hope because of your struggle with cancer. You kept moving forward, until cancer took you from us.

I admire how you took care of your mom and showed so much compassion. You went back to school, and you never gave up! Your short life was a testimony of courage and love – even in death, your light shined on.

Since you left the earth my dear friend, you have been my angel. You are my spiritual guide - even now... after more than 35 years have passed.

Anthony, I don't know where to start. It was 40 years later that I had a lump cut out of my breast and had chemo treatments, it wasn't until I was going through this, that I could try to feel how you felt. Scared, courageous, trying to move forward. I'm sure it was very hard - losing your leg and taking care of your mom and finishing college. You were very determined! You always had a ton of courage –

even when we were very little. Now, I understand more of what you went through. I was very fortunate to have found the lump so soon. Everyone will know about you now Anthony. Your kindness, love, friendship and your courage, Anthony, you are my angel now.

LESSONS

I learned so much from my friendship with Anthony:
1. True friendship - a true friend is someone who sticks by you through thick and thin and friendship is given on both sides. It is not self-absorbed, it is mutual. I was a child and learned this from my youngest friend.
2. Human connection – we become connected to the people in our lives. Even after you are away from someone you love, there are still connections. The connection was in my unconscious mind… Anthony was in my dreams, years after I had last seen him. Even my reconnection with Mary-Anna was a connection of more than fifty years in the making, God listened, and he led me. Anthony was in my dreams; he was also in my heart and soul.
3. Kindness, Understanding and Forgiveness - Anthony's mother, Mrs. Bonoma, showed true forgiveness. After an argument with her daughter, she kissed me on the check and spoke kindly. I choose not to harbor ill feelings, but I also don't need to be around them often. I can let go and not expose myself to poisonous people.
4. Fun - Life is short, take time to have some fun. We played ball, school, and Barbie almost every day. I learned to have fun early in life and it helped me later in life – when life was difficult, I remembered our fun-filled childhood days.

5. Death/loss – When Anthony died, I heard and saw the worse grief in the world. It is impossible to fully understand the pain and grief of losing a child and Anthony's death made me more open to my friend's pain when she lost her child.
6. Angel - Anthony has been my angel since he went into eternity. I talk to him and find comfort.
7. Compassion - Anthony showed compassion even at a young age When Mary-Anna and I would argue, he always remained calm and tried to soothe the situation.
8. Family - I loved being with family. I always felt the warmth, love and true friendship. Love – I always felt safe around Anthony's family. I felt love from them, even when I wasn't there.
9. Hope for the future - I learned hope. Hope is probably one of the most critical elements of survival. With hope, we can go on.
10. Perseverance - Anthony even helped me when I was healing from memories of childhood abuse - it was very hard, but I learned to keep moving forward. I have a life here - never give up! Anthony was gone way too soon - some people never have a chance to live their full life.

Do you have starlight times in your life, Dear Reader? Anthony, Mary-Anna and I had that time, even though it lasted for only a couple of years when we were very young! It is easy to take it for granted now, but it was a fun-filled time, we were young, life was easy and fun. We built connections and made solid relationships. Everyone has starlight times in their lives; my advice to you is to savor them! Even now, about 60 years later, I still cherish the time I shared with my childhood friends Anthony and Mary-Anna.

We were in our own world. Mary-Anna and I were always strong willed, and Anthony was kind – but not always kind to his sister – with Mary-Anna, he acted like a younger brother – he even tore off the head of her "tiny tears" doll! I looked forward to going to their house every day and I loved eating dinner with their family. I loved the nun outfits my mom made, and I loved the freedom of just being me and the joy of being alive!

I can still see the make-believe classroom that we played in for hours at a time. I can still see sweet Anthony sitting in his seat and smiling like a good student. I envision Mary-Anna and I in our nun outfits and taking turns being the teacher. Even today, I can still recall the smell of the roses and the smell of homemade red sauce. Mrs. Bonoma made all her food from scratch – these are the things which are always on my mind when I think of that starlight time.

After meeting up again on the internet after so many years - we were no longer children and it was long after Anthony was gone. Who would have thought that after all those years, we would meet up again - in Rome! Mary-Anna and John visited Rome for their 50th wedding anniversary at the same time my husband and I were celebrating our 45th wedding anniversary. I was so excited when we met up in the lounge. I had butterflies in my stomach! I can't even describe the excitement of knowing that we were doing this beautiful thing together. I am so happy we are back together again. Our time together in Rome was such a very special time. We had a beautiful Italian dinner together. We had time to sit and dine and talk – we talked about before and we talked about now; such a lovely night, such a lovely time, such a lovely place.

Afterword

Life has continued to be busy and life is moving on: Mary-Anna and I met in Rome and then we reconnected with our third-grade teacher.

We visited a recovery center on Saturday and had a Basilica trip on Sunday. We sat in the front pews; I let my third-grade teacher sit in the front with us (even though she had a senior citizen ticket). I went into the gift shop and purchased two gifts for my dear friend's young granddaughter, Marlee. I bought a book of saints and a bracelet from Padre Pio. Marlee has a brain tumor. I believe in miracles. I still believe Marlee can heal from this – even though the doctors said there is no way for Marlee to recover and they sent her home. I still believe God can do anything… so it is in His hands. And if not, I just want her to know we care. We are there for Marilee's family; they are all my dear friends, Kim, Vicky, Helene and Michelle. We turned around in the gift shop and saw Mary Anna, the three of us started hugging – it made me so happy to be there with Mary Anna and our third-grade teacher. I never thought this would happen in my lifetime. Anthony is looking down and can see us and he is happy.

On the left side of the altar is a picture of the Holy Family and the baby Jesus. I was so filled with love. I still have a statue of baby Jesus in my study. It was a gift from my mother. Mary Anna was on the altar, singing with the choir. My teacher Pat and my husband were sitting beside me, and Mary Anna's husband was sitting behind us – I just felt such joy, such utter and complete joy, I am praying that you, dear reader, will feel this joy many, many times in your lifetime.

This is my message – always see the beauty in life and always see the joy in life – even when it is very difficult, just a few days ago, Marlee lost her life. She was a little girl, who is up in heaven with Anthony now. Cancer took her life – she was only ten years old.

I have an appreciation for every day. I will help others heal and make it a better world. I was very young when I realized how hard it is to lose a loved one and it is especially hard to lose a child. My first experience of such grief was when I watched Mr. Bonoma after Anthony's funeral. Since then I have seen others lose children and it is so very painful. My friends: Carolyn, Marsha and Kim have lost their children. I have written of their grief and loss.

Where Have My Children Gone?
Losing Children

"We need to care for each other and love one another - for all the children that died, we need to honor them by living our lives and helping others. – Tell your family you love them every day. –DMM

I NEVER THOUGHT

I never thought I'd see in my lifetime what I always saw on TV. My friend's daughter was murdered. They still don't have all the details of what happened to the young, beautiful woman. I can't imagine the horrific pain my friend is feeling. Once again, it made me see what is important.

"Always try to see the beauty of each day" - I thought "how will I go to the funeral?". I just felt such compassion, such a despairing thought of going to the funeral and comforting my friend through this incredible suffering. I envisioned going to the funeral and being a comfort – but there is no comfort when there is complete and utter despair. I asked myself like I had so many other times "why God?"

I went to the church in Cape May, NJ and I prayed and lit candles to baby Jesus for my friend and others who need guidance. After living for 66 years, I had seen plenty and I understand pain – yet, this pain was incomprehensible. Now, the funeral is over, and my friend wants to join a foundation for domestic violence awareness and help people become more aware of this horrible crime -which happens every day. I just hope I can be a source of comfort and understanding. I don't know how and don't know where, but my heart opens for my friend. We share our feelings of pain over this tragedy. Isn't that the most important thing? To be there with an open heart and let others know you care. Sometimes it is not the giving of many things; it is just being present and listening - even though it is very hard to hear.

There are times when I speak to my friend and start crying, I can't fathom the loss my friend is experiencing. It is one thing for a child to die, it is another thing for a child to be murdered… I never thought it would be one of my friend's children. I never thought it would be so close to home.

Act like every day is the last day of your life. We don't know anything here. We just know that we need to be present in the days we have and open our hearts and minds to others. Enjoy your days and take time to see the beauty.

IT WAS A BEAUTIFUL MAY DAY
In Memory of Carolyn

It was a beautiful May Day
"How can it be so beautiful out here?" he said.
Yesterday she had a gun at the gun shot range.
"It still didn't hit me yet", he said.

Beautiful girl with torment and pain. . .
What did you do at the gun shot range?

"Dee Dee, I am so glad you came,
You were always so good to our Carolyn". . .
Beautiful girl with wrenching torment and cutting pain . . .
What did you do at the gun shot range?

Gunshot bullet to the brain…
That is what happened at the gun shot range!

Now… there are people left behind,
They love you and wonder why
There are feelings and questions
the human heart cannot explain.

Carolyn, you are out of your torment and pain,
This may be why you did what you did at the gun shot range.

I want people to know everywhere
Do not give in to your despair.
Suicide is final – there is no going back – I swear!

If you are living in torment and pain,
There are people who will see you through
And God's healing love is available too!

Please . . . In loving memory of Carolyn
July 1980 – June 2003 – Never give up!

WILTED FLOWER
(Marsha)

She said to me "today is the day I went through my daughter's closet and packed up all of her clothes, and I feel like a wilted flower". What can I say to her? Her pain is so, so deep.
I can't even imagine having to do that. I bet she really does feel like a wilted flower. So sad and so out of it and she will have better days and I will still be there for her. I will be there to let her know I really do care. I can't take away her pain, but I can listen.
I can't imagine how hard it is to lose your child. I imagine it feels like your heart being torn from your chest. I can hear it in her words and see it in her face. I will always listen…

WHERE

Where does someone's heart go when it judges the parents who have lost children in accidents or horrific ways? Their hearts are already broken from being unable to save their child. It is pain that cannot even be imagined – a misery like a knife, right through their soul!
I'll tell you where the judges go… to the depths of hell! I am screaming… "look into your own heart and see the truth… judgment is ice cold and ugly!"

I BELIEVE IN YOUR COMPASSION

There is a sadness –
I am crying.
There are children
who go through abuse
every day,
and there are children
who die.
BUT, crying
will not bring change,
standing up
with my courage
and resources
to do my part -
all I can…
to make a change
for a better world.
that is the answer.
I am not afraid,
to ask you
to join me.
Have a heart,
do your part,
big or small -
Help make a
brighter future
for children.
Let them know
that you care.
      I believe in your compassion.

FROM MY ESSAY: TIME FOR DISNEY

I've had enough reality this year! It is time for fantasy! I have reality every time I'm feeding my dad and he's calling me "mommy".
More reality every time I see tubes coming out of my sister-in-law Annie and more when I see and hear my friend grieving and crying asking "how am I going to live without my daughter?", and earlier in the year, losing our dear friend Michael… And my other friend who always thought her cheating-scum of a husband loved her, yet he has been with other women for years!
And now two of my favorite cousins died in one week - I will never see them on this earth again!
It is time for make believe - time for Disney!
2016 you need to go and 2017, I know you will be kinder.

This year has taught me plenty! My grandchildren are my joys and not mine to mold, they are mine to love, enjoy and spoil. That's what we grandparents are supposed to do! We have so much sharing and so much love! Laughing at grandpop with his bottom teeth out; laughing with my girls after my hat flew off on the monorail. I remember my son pushing me in a wheelchair and our time together because of my sore foot. I felt his love – thank you, son. Our meals and rides together are memories to hold in my heart forever.

Now as I am flying home I am asking myself what the answer is here. When I get annoyed or upset, I think "let it go", you are here and able to enjoy your life, while someone else is fighting for hers.
I have appreciation for this entire trip. I pray for more time together and I pray for more trips. How many more trips will we have like this? I enjoyed the random fits of joy in Disney World with my precious jewels. These fits of joy

will be in my heart, soul and mind for the rest of my life! When I get sad or angry, I will think of them! Thank you, God, for this precious time with my family!

Epilogue

I think Anthony really wants this book done. I am really trying my hardest. Mary Anna and I have been together many times since we were reunited. Right now, we are in Saint Bridget's church (est. 1853) where we made our sacraments and grew our faith.

I love this church and I always did. The windows are made of beautiful stained glass. It is so beautiful – even the windows and ceiling are full of charm and character. In this church, we prepared for our holy communion and our confirmation. We knelt and prayed and had the sacrament of penance; I felt the power of God so strongly… I still remember. There have been a few changes in the layout of the church… there used to be pews, but now there is a piano. We also prayed to St. Jude – the saint of the impossible.

I have so many wonderful memories of being in this church with my friends and praying. The Saint Peregrine statue is displayed above the candles. He is the patron saint of patients with cancer, aids or other illness. Saint Rita is also honored with a statue. I lit a candle for everyone in my life who needs prayer – my family and my friends. The lit candle is for all of you. It is time to leave, I am a woman of faith, I still picture us playing again in paradise.

Know that God is always there for you.

About the Author

Dolores M. Miller is a poet and author living in Pennsylvania with her Knight in Shining Armor, Larry, and together they have two grown children. The family has grown, and her four grandchildren are a source of joy and special inspiration. Dolores loves to move and dance and be free. Dolores loves life!

Proceeds from the books are donated to The Support Center for Child Advocates http://sccalaw.org/ Please contact them to see how you can get involved!

In 2018, Dolores was diagnosed with breast cancer. Her healing journey continued and the newest book "You Are Not Alone" will be published in 2021.

Dolores M. Miller

Poet, Author, Child Advocate and Inspirational Speaker

www.BeautifulWarrior.com
facebook.com/DoloresMMiller

"Please remember no matter what life brings to you, try to look at the positive side. It is your choice to enhance the good and let go of the bad. As a survivor I learned I do have choices. I choose to overcome and keep healing. I choose to become whole and become fully alive. My choice is life and to do all I can to make a better world." - DMM

www.ingramcontent.com/pod-product-compliance
Lightning Source LLC
LaVergne TN
LVHW041459070426
835507LV00009B/692